j 001.94
L337i

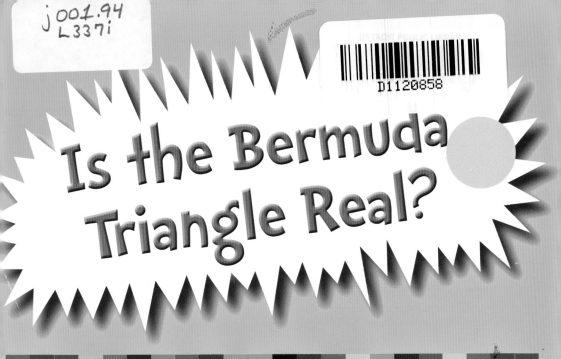

Is the Bermuda Triangle Real?

BY ALLISON LASSIEUR

CHANEY BRANCH LIBRARY
16101 GRAND RIVER
DETROIT, MI 48227

AMICUS HIGH INTEREST ✦ AMICUS INK

AUG 2016

Amicus High Interest and Amicus Ink are imprints of Amicus
P.O. Box 1329, Mankato, MN 56002
www.amicuspublishing.us

Copyright © 2016 Amicus. International copyright reserved in
all countries. No part of this book may be reproduced in any
form without written permission from the publisher.

Library of Congress Cataloging-in-Publication Data
Lassieur, Allison.
 Is the Bermuda Triangle real? / by Allison Lassieur.
    pages cm. – (Unexplained : what's the evidence?)
 Includes bibliographical references and index.
 Summary: "Presents stories of planes and ships that have
disappeared in the Bermuda Triangle, examining the
evidence of various explanations, ultimately stating that the
disappearances remain a mystery"–Provided by publisher.
 ISBN 978-1-60753-803-5 (library binding)
 ISBN 978-1-60753-892-9 (ebook)
 ISBN 978-1-68152-044-5 (paperback)
 1. Bermuda Triangle–Juvenile literature. I. Title.
 G558.L37 2016
 001.94–dc23

                                        2014033261

Series Editor   Rebecca Glaser
Series Designer   Kathleen Petelinsek
Book Designer   Heather Dreisbach
Photo Researcher   Derek Brown

Photo Credits: Shutterstock/irabel8, cover; Shutterstock/Alvov,
5; iStockphoto/Lightguard, 6; Corbis/Blue Lantern Studio,
9; Corbis /Bettmann, 10; U.S. Coast Guard, 13; National
Archives, 15; Shutterstock/Kisialiou Yury, 16; Shutterstock/
FloridaStock, 19; Alamy/Sergey Orlov, 20; Alamy/Arterra
Picture Library, 22; Alamy/Stocktrek Images, Inc., 25; Corbis/
Blend Images/Colin Anderson, 27; Shutterstock/Richard
Whitcombe, 28

Printed in Malaysia

HC 10 9 8 7 6 5 4 3 2 1
PB 10 9 8 7 6 5 4 3 2 1

Table of Contents

What Is the Bermuda Triangle?

The sea is calm. The air is clear. A ship sails in blue water. An airplane flies above the clouds. Then the ship is gone. The airplane is gone. They are never heard from again.

This might sound like a scary movie. But it is not. These things really did happen. They happened in a place called the Bermuda Triangle.

Could this ship disappear? Maybe, if it sails in the Bermuda Triangle.

Miami, Florida, is one point of the Bermuda Triangle.

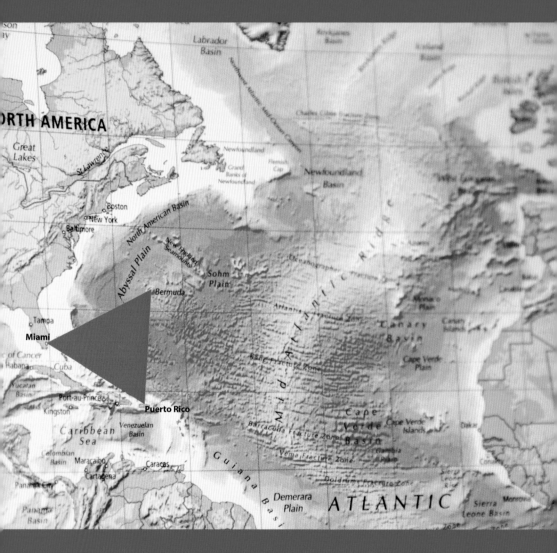

The Bermuda Triangle is in the Atlantic Ocean. It is not marked on any official maps. But you can find it. Connect Florida, Bermuda, and Puerto Rico. More than 70 boats and airplanes have disappeared in this area. Some people think there are **supernatural** forces here. Others don't believe them. Who is right?

 Yes. It is also called the Devil's Triangle and the Hoodoo Sea.

Mysteries at Sea

Christopher Columbus came to America in 1492. He sailed through the Bermuda Triangle. Strange things happened to his ships. He wrote about them in his journal. One day, the ship's **compass** did not point north. Days later, the sea was calm. There was no wind. Then a huge wave came up out of nowhere!

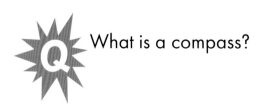 What is a compass?

Christopher Columbus sailed through rough waters in the Bermuda Triangle.

 A tool used to find your way. It has a magnetic needle that points north.

**The USS *Cyclops* carried
fuel for warships.**

 Did anyone from the *Cyclops* call for help?

The USS *Cyclops* was a navy **cargo** ship. In 1918, it sailed north from Brazil. It was on its way to Baltimore. More than 300 people were on board. The ship stopped at the island of Barbados. It was later seen sailing in the wrong direction. But after that, no one saw it. Did it disappear in the Bermuda Triangle? No one knows.

 No. After the ship left Barbados in good weather, no one heard from it again.

The SS *Marine Sulphur Queen* was a cargo ship. In 1963, it sailed from Texas. It disappeared in the Bermuda Triangle. Many teams looked for the ship. Finally they gave up. Then people on a navy ship near Key West, Florida, spotted a life jacket in the ocean. No one knows where the ship is.

Only a few objects from the *Sulphur Queen* were ever found.

The Lost Airplanes

One afternoon in 1945, navy pilots were training for war. Five planes were on a practice flight. It was called Flight 19. They flew over the Bermuda Triangle. At first, everything was fine. Then the flight leader called the base. He was lost. His compass had stopped working. The radio went dead.

Flight 19 was a bombing practice run. The pilots flew Avenger bomber planes like these.

The planes' compasses stopped working.

 Q What was the last radio message from Flight 19?

The radio came back on. But another pilot was talking. He said they were lost. The pilots were afraid. Their compasses stopped working, too. Nothing looked right. One of the pilots thought the leader was going the wrong way. The pilots asked for help. Then all five airplanes disappeared.

 It was: "We all go down together."

The navy looked for the airplanes. They did not find anything. There was no **wreckage**. They did not find anyone in the water. The lost planes were in the news. What was going on in the Bermuda Triangle? No one knew. To this day, no **trace** of the Flight 19 planes has been found.

 Was anything else strange about Flight 19?

Did Flight 19 crash in the swamps of the Florida Everglades? Some people looked there.

 One of the search planes disappeared, too. It was never seen again.

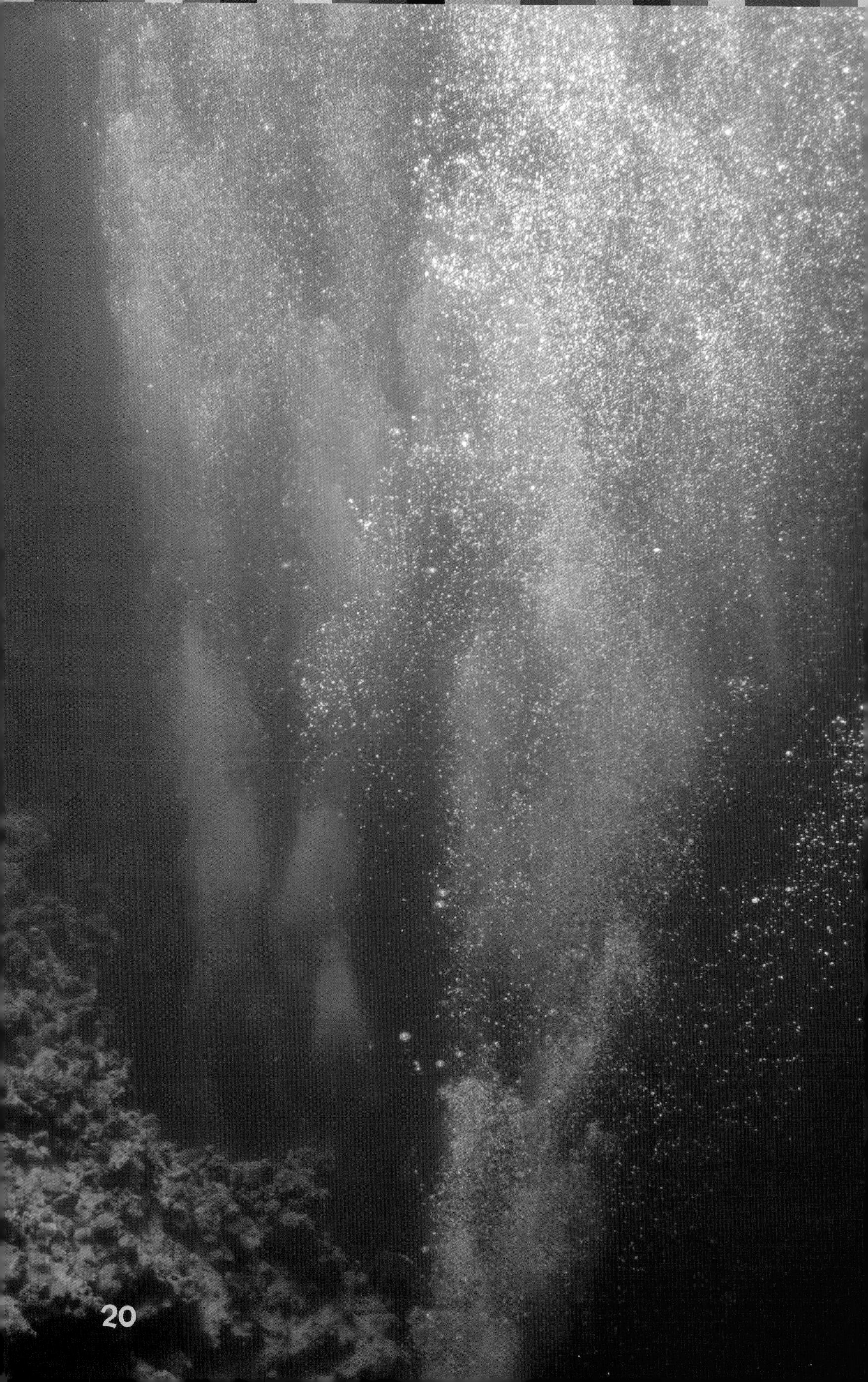

Mysterious Forces?

Since Flight 19, other planes and boats have vanished. There are lots of ideas to explain why. Some say it is underwater gas. Gas bubbles pop on the ocean surface. The bubbles are big enough to sink ships. Others say no. There is not enough gas to do any harm.

Gas bubbles rise to the ocean surface.

In 1970, Bruce Gernon was flying over the Bermuda Triangle. He saw a hole in a cloud and flew through it. His compass quit working. He landed in Miami. His trip should have taken 75 minutes. But it only took 47! Gernon said the hole was a tunnel through time. Today he calls the cloud "electronic fog." He says it causes ships and planes to disappear.

 Could electronic fog be real?

Can a hole in a cloud be more than a hole?

 Gernon says yes! But scientists say there is no such thing.

Could a comet explain the Bermuda Triangle?

Could **aliens** be stealing the ships and planes? That is one idea. Others say secret underwater testing is going on. Or an ancient **comet** might be to blame! They say a comet hit the earth thousands of years ago. It fell to the bottom of the ocean. Its energy causes compasses to stop working. So far, no one has proved any of these ideas are true.

What's the Evidence?

Are there supernatural forces in the Bermuda Triangle? There is no proof. Scientists say bad weather caused the ships and planes to disappear. Pilots and sailors could have made mistakes. The area has strong **currents**, winds, and thick fog. These could make ships sink or planes crash.

 Do all ships and planes go missing when they enter the Bermuda Triangle?

Many islands look the same from the air. It is easy to get lost.

 A No. Many ships and planes go through with no problems.

Plane wrecks are hard to find at the bottom of the sea.

But if ships sank or planes crashed, why are there no wrecks? The pieces might give us clues. Maybe the wrecks are so deep in the ocean that we can't find them. People still search. But so far, the Bermuda Triangle holds onto its secrets.

Glossary

alien A creature from another planet.

cargo Things carried by a ship or plane.

comet A bright object from space with a long tail of light.

compass A tool for finding directions that has a magnetic needle that points north.

current The movement of water in an ocean.

supernatural Something that cannot be explained by science.

trace A visible mark or sign that something has happened or that someone has been somewhere.

wreckage Broken parts of something that was destroyed.

Read More

Bingham, Jane. *Bermuda Triangle*. Chicago: Capstone Raintree, 2013.

Karst, Ken. *Bermuda Triangle*. Mankato, Minn.: Creative Education 2014.

Stewart, Melissa. *Is the Bermuda Triangle Really a Dangerous Place? : and Other Questions about the Ocean*. Minneapolis: Lerner, 2011.

Websites

KidzWorld: Scary Places: The Bermuda Triangle
www.kidzworld.com/article/1136-scary-places-4-the-bermuda-triangle

Naval Air Station Ford Lauderdale Museum: The Disappearance of Flight 19: Visual Exhibit
www.nasflmuseum.com/flight-19-exhibit.html

Science Kids: Earth Facts: The Bermuda Triangle
www.sciencekids.co.nz/sciencefacts/earth/bermudatriangle.html

Every effort has been made to ensure that these websites are appropriate for children. However, because of the nature of the Internet, it is impossible to guarantee that these sites will remain active indefinitely or that their contents will not be altered.

Index

About the Author

Allison Lassieur loves reading and writing about strange, mysterious, and unusual places in the world. She has written more than 150 books for kids, and she also likes to write about history, food, and science. Allison lives in a house in the woods with her husband, daughter, three dogs, two cats, and a blue fish named Marmalade.